The Artificial Intelligence Chatbot

Unexpected Positive Consequences

Lon Safko

Table of Contents

INTRODUCTION

Why Even Consider An A.I. Chatbot

Let's start by talking about what are the components of a successful, converting, revenue generating eCommerce web site: Assistance, Stickiness, Sales, and Revenue.

Assistance in helping the customers and prospects by answering whatever questions they have, asking about products, shipping, sizes, and other important support and pre-purchase questions.

Stickiness, to keep your prospects on the site long enough to build trust and convert them to customers, and customers, to convert them to repeat customers.

Sales, happen when the prospect or customer feels comfortable with the site, gets all their questions answered, find the product, service, or solution they were looking for and is eased through the shopping cart without issue. It's only then you can create a sale.

Revenue is when the customer is happy with the decision to purchase and the value of what they purchased, which generate word-of-mouth referrals, and customers that never return items and purchase more. The big question always is, how do you do that with your web site. That's what we will speak to in this "Pocket" book.

Whether your web site or Facebook page is based on eCommerce, Brick-&-Mortar Retail or other services, it is the time that your visitors spend on your site that directly correlates to revenue. If your visitors leave your site before their questions are answered, you will lose them and in most cases permanently. They will move on to another solution provider for their solution never to return.

We have gone to extraordinary lengths to determine how to keep our costly visitors on our sites. We have made an entire industry out of measuring "eye-gaze", A&B testing copy, colors, and images, WordPress Classic versus the new Block designs, layouts, pop-ups, menus, click-thru rates, and a lot more, all to find that perfect balance of aesthetics, content, and ease of use that converts.

Historic Reference

For historical reference, you can find my biography here: www.Safko.com/about and my news and background site here: www.LonSafko.com

In addition to what my bio shows, I programmed one of the very first A.I. chatbots ever back in 1978. I started with an "Eliza" [1] (referenced below), kernel and greatly expanded on it until I had also created the rudimentary components of what is now called today, "Machine Learning" [2]. With a computer that only contained 48k of RAM (expanded), it was pretty sophisticated for its day. While it would never have passed the "Turing Test" [3], it was pretty amazing for its time and I did sell a lot of copies of it.

Below are three Wikipedia links to the foundational concepts mentioned above. This paper is not designed to speak to these specific concepts, but you might find the historical value and components an interesting read for background.

[1]: https://en.wikipedia.org/wiki/ELIZA

[2] : https://en.wikipedia.org/wiki/Machine_learning

[3]: https://en.wikipedia.org/wiki/Turing_test

In 1978, the software then named "Let's Talk", would take input from a keyboard, actually speak aloud its responses. When it didn't understand the conversation or question, it would ask the user to please explain the proper response. It would then learn from that interaction and store that information for later retrieval. The next time that subject was discussed by the user, it would then give the correct answer.

Eventually, I added voice recognition so it could hear the user speak, convert the speech to text, input that text, and respond through its own voice. This was the first fully functional two-way voice communication that could control all of the computer functions along with the telephone and a full range of environmental controls (255 separate lamps and appliances.)

By 1985, this system became my product known as "SoftVoice", which is considered to be the "First Computer To Save A Human Life" coined by Steve Jobs, and now resides in the Smithsonian Institution in Washington, D.C. along with 18 other inventions and 30,000 professional papers. I also have 14 inventions in the Computer History Museum in Mountain View, California based on this series of products.

What Is An A.I. Chatbot

An A.I. chatbot is essentially a two-way text chat between a prospect / customer / human and an algorithm, a computer code, an app. It has the initials name A.I. or Artificial Intelligence, preceding its name because the computer app, mimics the intelligence of a human communicating through text. The text is being read through the input from the user, the app identifies keyword(s) in the sentence, looks those word(s) up in a table, and texts (or speaks) back the predetermined coded response based on the word(s) identified. As an example:

If the User says, "Good morning." The app looks up the phrase "good morning", identifies the phrase in a list of possible responses (Linked-Lists), randomly chooses one, and returns "And, good morning to you!", or "How are you on this fine morning?" And, the conversation continues.

> *Note: This a rule-based chatbot. Most chatbot platforms on the market today only support rule-based. To identify a rule-based chatbot, check to see if it allows free text input and gives a reasonable response when you enter any text.

The Machine-Learning aspect of a chatbot is, when the bot is faced with a keyword(s) that has not been pre-identified and programmed, it either has to ask the user to explain, or searches the Internet for a corresponding answer, and respond according. How well it responds denotes the quality and usability of that particular chatbot. The better the answers returned, the more useful the chatbot is. A self-learning AI chatbot can try to discover information from external resources like web pages to answer questions that it's never asked or taught before.

If the chatbot can fool a human into thinking they are actually chatting with another human, then that chatbot is considered to have passed the Turing Test. See footnote[4] above.

Nearly all chatbots today do not learn. Every response has to be individually thought out, created, and programmed in. this makes a one size chatbot fits all, very difficult as the content on every website can be significantly different along with the products, and types of questions asked by prospects and customers. Programming most chatbots can be very difficult and could require software programming experience.

Many of the newer more sophisticated chatbot platforms provide "visual development" tools; however, that doesn't mean they are development-free. While the users don't need to work with codes, they still need to design the chatflow, which is the core task of developing a chatbot and requires remarkable efforts.

The chatbot I am featuring in the book does learn on its own. More about this soon. It scans the entire web site every 24 hours and re-indexes all the pages, content, and products. The chatbot learns not from user input, but from the site's content itself. We cannot trust the users to teach our chatbots appropriate responses. Microsoft recently ran an experiment using the social network, Twitter. It turned out disastrous and was forced to be shut down in under 16 hours. Here's the first paragraph summary about Microsoft's "Tay" from Wikipedia:

Tay was an artificial intelligence chatter bot that was originally released by Microsoft Corporation via Twitter on March 23, 2016; it caused subsequent controversy when the bot began to post inflammatory and offensive tweets through its Twitter account, forcing Microsoft to shut down the service only 16 hours after its launch. According to Microsoft, this was caused by Trolls who "attacked" the service as the bot made replies based on its interactions with people on Twitter. It was soon replaced with Zo.

Wikipedia: https://en.wikipedia.org/wiki/Tay_(bot)

What Microsoft didn't say in the statement above, is that Tay learned from the interactions with its human counterparts by tweeting, and retweeting and as one reporter called Microsoft's chatbot, Tay, "a racist asshole in less than a day". His words, not mine. Here's the article:

https://bit.ly/2u8m6qB

This just proves once again, humans cannot be trusted, unsupervised.

Choosing The Right A.I. Chatbot

There is a myriad of chatbots all with different purposes. Some are designed for tech support, some product recommendations, some to gather information from a such as "how do you like our website", and some are designed to capture email addresses to generate leads. Choosing the right A.I. chatbot depends on what do you want to accomplish with your A,I. chatbot.

I looked at dozens of A.I. chatbot applications and plug-ins available today. The one I chose was Aco from www.Acobot.ai. It was by far, the very best A.I. chatbot I tested. This is after studying and installing more than a dozen A.I. chatbots available for my WordPress web sites and comparing how easy they were to install, how they performed, and most importantly, how they learned.

While overall performance is paramount, the biggest key factor was the initial set up. Acobot.ai was a quick WordPress plug-in installation with only a couple of clicks, while many of the others were more than awful! Many required hours of set-up, designing flowcharts, and actually, make us the user, developing every possible keyword input and response. In most cases, you needed to be a software programmer, which made them unusable.

Acobot.ai, once installed, scanned my site, found keyword on every page, and identified every one of my more than 100 products along with all of their descriptions, the Frequently Asked Questions page, the Tips & Tricks page all in less than 24 hours. I was amazed to see that a day after the installation, Acobot.ai. was able to answer all of my visitor's most difficult questions the first time!

Note: Let me make it clear, I do not work for Acobot.ai, I am not affiliated with Acobot.ai, I have never been paid by them and I am not an affiliate marketer receiving any compensation whatsoever. This statement is in accordance with the guidelines set forth by the F.C.C. and the F.T.C. This is not a sponsored publishing.

There are many types of chatbots each designed of a specific purpose. The type of A.I. chatbot I installed and analyzed herein was designed to be a lead generation chatbot. Its primary purpose is to capture email addresses or telephone numbers. Its secondary purpose is to provide customer support, product identification, and general assistance.

This particular A.I. chatbot is very versatile and easy to change its settings. Some of the options are "Name", you can call it anything you wish and from that point on, it will refer to itself by that name.

You can change its "Avatar" or the image it uses as its face. Widget style is another option whereby it can be rounded corners and without, classic or modern, you choose. You can also choose the widget color, type of leads; telephone, and / or email, and you can do it either by text chatting or through a dozen or more human sounding voices. Most of the options are just a click.

I took the time to list these options because most people have no idea how versatile a well-designed A.I. chatbot can be. And, there is importance to these settings which you will read about further down.

Meet Bella, My A.I. Chatbot

I would like to introduce you to "Bella" my A.I. chatbot. Or, feel free to meet and interact with Bella yourself by visiting:

www.PaperModelsOnLine.com

I designed Bella to appear to be a young, female-voiced* puppy dog to capture email addresses, locate products, and answer support questions all using the options above. I chose this configuration because our web site sells downloadable school products.

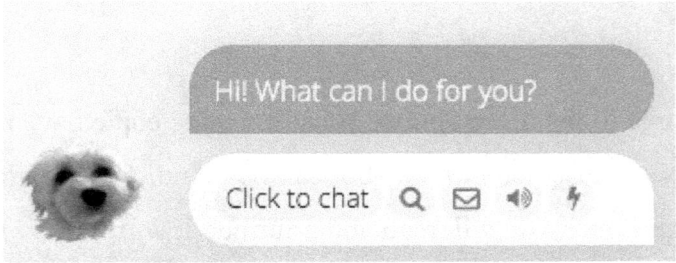

Note: Have you ever noticed, nearly all A.I. Voice Assistants speak in a female voice. All of them from Alexa, to Siri, Cortana, to the GPS in your car. Dr. Thomas Furness considered the Father of Virtual Reality while working at the Wright-Patterson Air Force Base nearly 40 years ago developed the first V.R. discovered that the pilots responded best to a female A.I. voice.

*Note within a Note: V.R. stands for Virtual Reality. Here is a link to the Wikipedia page that will explain what the means:

https://en.wikipedia.org/wiki/Virtual_reality

Back to female voice. Here are several statements from major Voice Assistant manufacturers:

Amazon
"We tested many voices with our internal beta program and customers before launching and this voice tested best," an Amazon spokesperson told PC Magazine. And…

Microsoft
A Microsoft spokesperson said Cortana can technically be genderless, but the company did immerse itself in gender research when choosing a voice and weighed the benefits of a male and female voice. "However, for our objectives—building a helpful, supportive, trustworthy assistant—a female voice was the stronger choice," according to Redmond.

Be aware, the right choice of avatar image and voice depends on the subject matter of the website and your audience. I joke when teaching this, that women don't mind taking instructions from other women while men are expecting it. I know sexist. Sorry!

On the Paper Models, Inc. web site, we provide downloadable pdf files of popular school projects, volcanos, the White House, the Alamo, and for the State of California, we cater to mostly 4th graders (9-year-olds), who are required to build one of the 21 California Missions to represent the state's history. We also include the history summary of the landmark / subject so the kids can write their reports. As this site caters to parents, teachers, but especially kids, I chose the puppy and child voice. And, it worked.

On my other sites, my professional speaking web site www.Safko.com and my Biography web site www.LonSafko.com, I have an anime female image (Eve from WALL-E the Disney animated movie) with an adult female voice. I could have chosen a graphic female image or even uploaded a photo of my choice, but I still wanted to keep the chatbot fun,

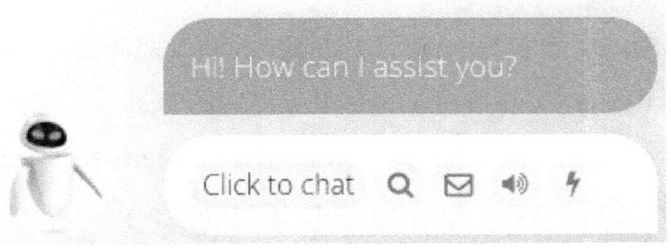

so I chose Eve.

Immediately after I switched the www.PaperModelsOnLine.com avatar from an adult to an avatar that is appealing to a younger audience, I found the number of engagements and interactions went up dramatically, and of course, so did the sales / revenue. I think the younger appeal comes across as less intimidating and more friendly to the younger audience. The longer you can keep your visitor to stay on your page, the more they engage, the more they trust, the more they buy.

Here are some actual numbers from that chatbot. For the first 120 days (a 4 month) period since I installed the Acobot.ai on www.PaperModelsOnLine.com, I saw more than 2,000 Sessions (the number of unique user conversations) with 22,802 Interactions take place.

The ratio between Sessions and Interactions on average was 11.4 Interactions per Session. That means, on average, that every prospect and customer that came to my web site, interacted with the chatbot a minimum of 11 times! That's a lot more interactions than your visitors click out of your web site once they encounter your annoying pop-ups. There was even one Session that lasted for 104 Interactions!

The developer of Acobot.ai has shared with me that for one customer, in only 150 days, the Aco chatbot captured 19,151 email addresses / new sales leads. Of course, this based on the amount of overall site traffic volume, but this is the largest scale of lead generation by chatbot I ever heard of. More impressive, Aco converted 18.7% of users who ever interacted with it into sales leads for that customer.

UNEXPECTED POSITIVE CONSEQUENCES

The biggest surprises came from actually reading the conversations between my prospects / customers and the chatbot. They were so amazing, that's why I wanted to write this book to share them with you. You would never expect to see such unexpected positive consequences of just installing a chatbot. Hence, the name of the book.

Making Your Site "Sticky"

The term "sticky" when discussing web sites, in particular, home pages refers to the amount of time a visitor stays on the web site's page. The idea is that the longer you can keep the prospect on the site, the more time they have to discover something they need /want, the greater they trust you and your site, and the higher probability they will purchase from you.

Keeping your visitor on your web site is no easy task. One wrong image, one lengthy paragraph, one broken link, one pull-down menu, or just if the visitor loses interest, they are gone. Most likely, gone forever. All the work and expense you incurred to get them there, is now lost.

When a web site visitor comes to your home page the visitor makes a 10-second judgment, call. Visitors will often look around a bit but are highly likely to leave during the subsequent 20 seconds of initial their visit. Only after people have stayed on a page for 30 seconds or more, does the exit curve become relatively flat. Think about it… What do you do?

I found with Acobot.ai, the rate of interactions is significantly higher than any optimization I have ever done with a web site. While many of the chats last 5 to 10 minutes, some documented chats lasted over 1,500 seconds or 25 minutes! This is causing your prospects to imprint their memories with your web site for longer periods of time, making the connection between them, you, and your product significantly stronger. That hasn't been anything I have tried over the past 20 years that has caused that significant of a change. A pop-up won't keep your visitor engaged on your web site for 25 minutes.

The visitor is just more comfortable chatting with a bot than trying to navigate your site to find what they are looking for. The chatbot answers the most frequently asked questions which makes them happy with the web site, when they do leave, usually after the sale.

Question: Ask yourself this "How many people leave your web site within the first 30 seconds angry, never to come back because they could find what they were looking for?" Acobot.ai will engage with them in a friendly, helpful manner answering questions and keeping them on your site longer. The chatbot will actually turn frustrated visitors into happy customers.

Annoying Pop-Ups

Acobot.ai certainly is a lot more effective than the annoying web site Pop-Ups that ask you to enter your email for the next newsletter. The last web site I was looking at, I was there reading when one of those pops-up, popped-up. As quickly as I could, I closed that page. I suddenly realized that was what I do every time a pop-up, pops-up and you know you do the same thing.

So, why do you think your web visitor is any different? If you ever want to know what your web site visitor thinks of something, be honest and ask your self how you feel when you encounter the same experience.

Like everyone else, I created that type of pop-up for several of my WordPress web sites. The following day, when I encountered the pop-up asking me for my email that I describe above, I closed that window, opened all of my web sites, and deleted all of the pop-ups I had created the day before. We all hate them. They don't work. So, don't use them.

If by using your pop-up, you are experiencing good conversion (attaining the visitor's email address) or if it has increased your visitor's time on the site, please contact me with your first-hand experiences and I will amend this section. Of all the people I interviewed, their conversion rate has been very low to zero and the time the visitor spends on the site is low as well.

Acobot.ai uses popups to engage users too. I disabled it at beginning because I hate popups so much. Several weeks later I re-enabled it unexpectedly and found the user sessions surged about 20%. Another big surprise! When looked more closely at this feature I discovered: Acobot.ai uses a one-time popup for users who're leaving but haven't interacted with it yet. Aco just says hello and offers help to users. I think that's why many users responded because a "Conversational pop-up" does work!

Contact Forms

What I found was, people will use the chatbot when they won't use the contact form. During the same 120-day observation period, with more than over 2,000 chatbot customer Engagements, I experienced only 6 contact form engagements. I found this astonishing.

All of my sites, like every other site on the web, has a "contact" form, which is available from the main menu above the folder. It always surprised me that with the high volume of traffic to my site, I always had so very few inquiries through the contact form; nearly none. I just assumed that I must have done such a terrific job designing the web site and that my Frequently Asked Question (FAQ) page must have been amazing. Turns out I was wrong.

Immediately after installing the A.I. chatbot, I started receiving dozens of questions each week. Sometimes five or six in a day. While 80% of the questions were, addressed in the FAQ page and the chatbot answered them correctly, I found that approximately 20% or more weren't unanswerable based on the web sites total content. In fact, of that 20%, I never thought of those particular questions. As an example: "If I order using USPS Priority Shipping today, how long would it take to get to me?"

It never crossed my mind that this was a pressing question my customer had as this wasn't a function of my company. We always mail the same day, while the rest is up to the United States Postal Service. I just assumed that people knew how long the Post Office took to ship. We clearly list the two standard options; Priority and Express.

As a result of reading that question so often in the chatbot chat-logs, for the first time I came upon two more discoveries; one is that in the 20 years of operation, I never realized that my prospects had that question and another they would never use the contact form to ask it.

About 1 out of 4 times and adult asked a question to the chatbot, they provided their email address so we could contact them immediately. This nearly always leads to an immediate purchase that we never would have made. One chatbot conversation specifically said the user would not buy until they got this answer. She left her email address, I was able to respond within minutes, and she purchased moments later. Sale saved.

As the product mix on this site is school projects, timing is everything. A majority of our clients (parents) download our projects Sunday afternoon only after cleaning out their child's backpack and discovering their child's project is due Monday morning! If you have kids, you know exactly what I am talking about.

Not knowing they can select an instant download or 2-4 days USPS shipping, I am sure, has prevented my customers from purchasing more than I care to admit, now. Over the two decades, I can only imagine how much revenue I lost over that period because of an oversight as simple as this.

And again, within 24 hours, the chatbot found the new paragraph I added about the shipping options and delivery times on the FAQ page, indexed it, and was able to answer that very question the next day for a client perfectly, most likely saving the sale once again. There is also an option whereby you can request an immediate update or rescanning of the site if you need to get something urgent into effect as soon as possible.

All this made me wonder why, with the "contact" in the clearly displayed in the menu, no one would ever use it. So, I analyzed this also. After questioning dozens of my existing customers, they told me, they never use any web site contact forms, because they know that's the way companies capture email address for their Spam lists.

In addition, some customers don't want to use contact form because they think their questions are too trivial to be worthy of an "official" communication, while other customers have a disappointing experience of a very slow or no responses when they use a contact form. This is especially true with large companies. Little did they know, that the Acobot.ai chatbot was specifically designed to do just that; capture prospects email addresses.

When the visitors interacted with Acobot.ai., they felt they could do it anonymously without fear of compromising their email addresses to a Spam list. Acobot.ai is more than 300 to 1 better than a contact form.

This wasn't obvious to me either as every one of my web sites are U.S. CAN SPAM Act* and GDPR* compliant and has a full "Privacy Policies" page that promises I would never sell your address or use it to harass you with spam. Just like the FAQ page, this is another page that our prospects and customers refuse to read.

[1] CAN-SPAM Act of 2003:
www.en.wikipedia.org/wiki/CAN-SPAM_Act_of_2003
[2] GDPR (General Data Protection Regulation):
www.EUGDPR.org

This is another observation where the A.I. chatbot showed me that the contact form which we all rely on is useless and does not perform its function. This is also another way, we all are losing customers (revenue) every single day. This is especially true for the businesses who solely rely on a contact forms, email addresses or telephone numbers to generate sales leads. They don't work well regardless how interesting the call-to-action is.

Coupons & Discount Codes

When I teach my advanced marketing courses and we get to the Coupon / Discount segment, I always start out by saying that I am not a big fan of coupons or discount codes. In my opinion, they are just a way of leaving money on the table, a lot of money.

The intent of using a coupon is to convert a prospect into a first time customer. It's designed to entice them to try your product at a discount. When that happens, the revenue lost on each coupon is a very inexpensive way to gain a new customer. That's called the Cost of Customer Acquisition (CoCA). With most company's CoCA being in the hundreds of dollars per actual customer, the small discount provided by the coupon is negligible and well worth the cost; However...

Most of the people who use your coupons already know about your product. They aren't first time buyers or prospects converting to customers. They are repeat customers who are using your coupons to save money for themselves by taking it from your revenue stream. They would have purchased your product at full price anyway. That's just giving up revenue without any Return On Investment. (R.O.I).

I also found an interesting psychological divide. After studying so many conversations between my A.I. and two thousand prospects, I began to notice a subtle difference; some people, a small percent would simply "ask" the A.I. if I offered any type of a coupon or discount. I didn't because of my previous research that I presented above. But, the requests persisted.

This caused me to think about why some prospects ask for coupons and so many do not. The A.I. allowed me to understand that when it comes to coupons and discounts, prospects fall into two different categories, the ones that are psychologically motivated by getting a "deal" or a "discount" which is really important to them, while the other category of prospects simply can't be bothered, they just don't care.

We see this in the grocery stores checkout lines. Nearly every shopper couldn't care less about saving 10¢ on that next can of cat food, while there is always that "coupon lady" who seems to be in the checkout line right in front of me. Why do I always choose that line?

This created fundamental a dilemma for me. I now understand that coupons are really motivational to some prospects and I didn't want to lose them. I also didn't want everyone to just take a percentage off the retail price. What to do?

I decide to take advantage of my new A.I. and created a simple post with only the title "10DOAPAT" and the content "Use this coupon code 10DOAPAT to receive your 10% Discount On Any Product Any Time!" That's it. It was published as "Uncategorized" so you couldn't find it in the Blog. it was essentially, invisible to the web site visitor.

Within 24 hours, my A.I. chatbot, Aco, found the new post page, indexed it, and that morning created this conversation.

Aco: How can I assist you?

User: Any coupons or discounts right now?

Aco: Are you asking about: what is your discount code?

User: Yes

Aco: Use the code "10DOAPAT" to receive your 10% Discount On Any Product, Any Time! Or, could you please give me your email address? We will get back to you with further information you need.

Acobot.ai, gave the correct answer to the specific prospect who needed it at the specific moment necessary to close the sale. 15 minutes later, I saw the notification that this prospect converted to a customer and purchased the product.

For the people who aren't motivated by coupons, they don't see one, they don't ask for one. For the people that are motivated by discounts and savings, is given the information immediately and they think they beat the system. They grab the code and close the sale.

The coupon is for 10% off. While most of our products retail for $9.95, in this case, my cost of customer acquisition is only 99¢. This is well worth getting the $10 sale. The chatbot served it up perfectly at just the right moment to just the right prospect, and no one else.

> *Note: Alternatively, you can use Acobot's FAQ feature to implement similar functionality. This feature allows you to teach Aco to answer any questions that you don't want to add to your web site.

Bad Content Was Damaging Sales

What would you think if your chatbot was directing your (valuable) prospects to your competitor's web site, without your knowledge? It happened to me! I discovered that it wasn't through the fault of A.I. It was my fault for added that content to my web pages. Acobot.ai gave me a great chance to recognize this and improve my web site's content.

I had too many external links to competing products and web sites and didn't realize it. As mentioned above, on this web site there is a Tips & Tricks blog page to help parents and students the basics of building a mission from scratch if they either don't want to buy my kits or kits not allowed to be used. This page had movies, books, photos, and links to Amazon books and other web pages.

When Acobot.ai was asked about how to build a California Mission school project, it gave the prospect the link I provided several years ago when I wrote the content for Tips & Tricks and How To Build A California Mission Project pages, to a competitors web site. This link took my customer away from my site and caused them to buy a competitor's product. The page was originally designed to help the user find additional resources not reduce my revenue. I had no idea that it was there cause this kind of a problem.

When I re-read the page, I realized I were making it way too easy to drive our customers to Amazon and buy a book instead of purchasing my products. So... I went through the web site and removed all the links to Amazon and other people's products, kept the page as a helpful resource, and added more non-competing helpful information. It sounds obvious now, but at the time, I was trying to be helpful, and completely forgot the information was there taking my customers to another place to buy.

This was another major insight that the Acobot.ai chatbot inadvertently made me aware of. It is a major problem I would have never discovered without the chatbot.

Improve the Web Site Content

The web site has several "help" pages for the parents, students, and teachers which include "Tips & Tricks", "How To", and "FAQ" pages. Over the past four months of using the chatbot, I have seen questions asked that I never would have anticipated even after 20 years in business with our eCommerce web site. If the user gave the Bot their email address I would, as quickly as possible, respond directly to that user. I then added that question and answer to the "FAQ" page. Once again, within 24 hours, AcoBot.ai would continuously rescan the site, find the new information and immediately offer that new information to my customers and prospects.

As a result of running the chatbot for the previous four months, the FAQ page has become quite robust and every single question my visitors now ask, AcoBot.ai answers immediately and correctly.

Help Customers Identify Products

Connecting the customer directly to the product they were looking for was a terrific unexpected consequence.

The web site traffic has always been high volume, but the conversion has always been very low. The actual number of sales, when compared to the number of visitors, represented a very small percentage of the visits.

In the 2,000+ chatbot conversations, the most frequently asked question is turned out to be: Where can I find…"

When a customer comes to our web site, they usually know what they are looking for. The project has been assigned by a teacher or it is the subject of the current curriculum. Even though I try to make the web site logically organized, easy to navigate, and have a search function, finding the one product they are looking for out of 100^+, it still takes time that web visitors don't want to spend.

I have watched as the customer is greeted by Acobot.ai and the first thing they ask is "Where can I find...". Most visitors don't want to take the time to look around the web site. They don't want to navigate through pages of the 100^+ products to find the one they are looking for. They are like us; they don't have time or the inclination to "browse." They know what they want and they want it now.

When asked, Aco immediately says "Oh, you are looking for this... Click here." The chatbot automatically brings the customer to the exact product page the customer was looking for. This has led to a dramatic 30% increase in sales / revenue every month for the four months the chatbot has been installed. It's worth repeating, I have increased my revenue by 30% over the same months last year for every month it has been installed.

Here's an example of just one of the many of this type of question asked of the Bot.

Aco:	Hello! How can I assist you?
User:	I am trying to locate and build the notre dame cathedral
Aco:	Are you asking about: NOTRE DAME?
Aco:	www.PaperModelsOnline.com/Product/Notre-Dame-Chathedral

While providing the direct link, the chatbot actually opened the web page for the customer.

When the chatbot conversations like this one come into my email, I watch the sales emails. Inevitably, within 10 to 15 minutes, I see that prospect purchased that product.

The technical term for that is called "Cha-Ching!"

Identify prospect Demographic

Our Web Site Demographic Was 100%… Incorrect

Even after 20 years this of managing and developing this web site and product line, the chatbot showed me that I didn't know what I didn't know when it came to my customers. Of course, you would think, being a school project eCommerce web site, the typical customer was the parent, maybe the occasional teacher. You know, the ones with the credit cards. Who else could it be?

Well, it turned out that showed me that 95% of our web site traffic were kids! Fourth graders, 9-year-olds, were looking for solutions on how they could build their California Mission project, not parents, not teachers. It was 9-year olds. That finally explained why our visit rate was always so high, but our conversion rate has always been so low.

It was kids, not parents. Kids, the ones without the credit cards. Once I learned this, I quickly realized that the 9-year-olds would come to the site, find our downloadable project solution for under $10, and run to get their parents who came to the web site only to verify and make the purchase with their credit card.

Without A.I., I would have never figured this out. 20 years and I hadn't figured it out up until now. This alone is a huge reason to install an A.I. chatbot on every site. I had it wrong all those years and no other technology could have shown me the truth. It's true, you don't know, what you don't know.

Knowing My Customers Location

Finally, after reviewing so many conversations (2,000+), I suddenly have a clear picture for the first time of the exact geographic areas where my prospects are coming from. Every Engagement notification says as closely as can be determined, where the web site visitor is coming from.

Web site tracking services like Google Analytics may provide your with geographic data; however, they're overall summary numbers where you cannot associate them with the specific user and their behavior.

Hey there

Bella has Interacted with a User from Los Angeles, United States

Review this log to better understand your customers, enhance your website, and boost sales!

This now helps me target the types of ads and especially the geo-location of where my ads should be placed. I can tell from this information, where my geographical 'hot spots" are at any given time not only saving me a great deal of ad-rev (advertising revenue), but making the ad-rev I do spend significantly more effective, decreasing my Cost of Customer Acquisition, and returning multiples in additional profit.

CONCLUSION

I am sure when you began reading this you had a very strong negative opinion of chatbots in general. I know I did. That's why I needed to find out for myself. As you can see, I was amazed at eh Unexpected Positive Consequences of installing a chatbot.

Even the visitors to your web site will most likely have a negative preconceived opinion the chatbot before the ever interact with it. Once they do, they will see how unintimidating and helpful a chatbot can be.

Remember when running your own trial of your A.I. chatbot, if it is a good as the chatbot, you will need to give it time to learn the content of your web site. Also, the chatbot cannot answer any questions that your web site doesn't discuss. Be patient and help it for the first few weeks by adding unanswered questions to your FAQ page. Give the Bot a chance to learn.

Don't get discourage if the A.I. fails to answer some questions. There are always the occasional question that A.I. cannot answer but that doesn't prevent Acobo.ai from converting more visitors into leads and sales.

And, don't get disappointed if most people still will not give their very guarded email address over to a strange chatbot. It's a matter of fact it's not every visitor to your website is ready to buy your products or services at that very moment. Most of your visitors are browsing and may not be interested in your product or service at that moment.

Observe the number of visitors that do give their email addresses the chatbot compared to the number of email addresses you were getting from your contact form or your popups.

While installation is significantly easier than all of the other chatbots I tested, there still is some setup. The good news is they've added a wizard to walk you through the setup. Be patient with this as well. The result will be well worth your effort.

Setting the AcoBot.ai ChatBot up is like doing anything else for the first time, it is foreign but logical. Once you go through the process, you will consider yourself an expert.

>*Note: The most tricky setting is to determine is what web pages do you want your chatbot to index and what pages do you not. I was confused with that at first, but figured it out with the help of Acobot support. I recommend you turn to them directly for optimizing that option and saving you that time.

Your lead generation will increase. The developer of the Acobot.ai has seen their customers leads increase between 30% to 100%. Fact: My sales and revenue went up 30% and I generated more sales leads with Acobot.ai than any other method I have tried over the past 20 years.

The developer has also shared that many of their customers who previously used live chat, which is expensive for the required human resources, found that Acobot.ai delivered more leads at only a fraction of the cost. Some of them even have put both Acobot.ai and live chat on the website at the same time. They found that the A.I. has achieved a higher conversion rate for lead generation than did the more expensive live chat.

Based on all of the above research and more than 2,000 Sessions and 22,800 Interactions between my prospects / customers, I am now overwhelmingly in favor of using an A.I. chatbot on all of my web sites and strongly recommend that you consider doing the same.

In only four months, I found that the chatbot:

- Increased my visitors time on my site from 20 seconds to over 25 minutes in many cases.
- Collected significantly more email addresses / sales leads than did my pop-ups causing me to eliminate them.
- Built trust with my prospects and customers more than the contact form.
- Collected email addresses at a rate of 300 to 1 when compared to my contact form.
- Answered critical prospect questions that immediately lead to sales.
- Significantly reduced customer support by delivering answers to my customers.

- Could deliver discount coupons to only the prospects that needed them to close the sale.
- Identified bad content which was causing my visitors to buy from my competitors.
- Allowed me to identify important questions my customers wanted, but I had no idea was important.
- Assisted me in improving the content of all my web pages, especially my Frequently Asked Questions (FAQ) page.
- Allowed prospects to connect to their desired product with one click, thus increasing the closure rate and revenue.
- Showed me I was wrong about my visitor demographics and identified the correct profile.
- Allowed me to identify the geographic locations of my prospects to more accurately develop efficient ad-spends, saving me thousands of dollars. And…
- Increased my revenue every month since it was added to the web site.

In conclusion, among the dozens of chatbots I've tested, by far, Acobot.ai works best.

If you found this information helpful, please drop me an email and let me know at LonSafko@LonSafko.com!

Thank you!

Author • Speaker • Trainer

www.Safko.com • www.LonSafko.com

www.ingramcontent.com/pod-product-compliance
Lightning Source LLC
Chambersburg PA
CBHW072309170526
45158CB00003BA/1250

* 9 7 8 1 0 7 0 9 7 9 6 5 6 *